House Under the Moon

# Also by Michael Sowder

*The Empty Boat*
*Whitman's Ecstatic Union*
*A Calendar of Crows*

March 4, 2013

To Chris,

Great to meet you at Mount
Mercy.
Thanks for reading my

book.
Good luck with your career.

Michael

# House
## Under the Moon

Michael Sowder

New Odyssey Series
Truman State University Press
Kirksville, Missouri

Cover art: "Light of the Moon," by Chelsea Barg. Used with permission.

Cover design: Teresa Wheeler

Library of Congress Cataloging-in-Publication Data
Sowder, Michael, 1956–
House under the moon / Michael Sowder.
    p. cm. — (New odyssey series)
ISBN 978-1-61248-058-9 (pbk. : alk. paper) — ISBN 978-1-61248-059-6 (ebook)
I. Title.
PS3619.O96H68 2012
811'.6—dc23
                                                      2012030593

*Something mysteriously formed,*
*Born before heaven and Earth.*
*In the silence and the void,*
*Standing alone and unchanging,*
*Ever present and in motion.*
*Perhaps it is the mother of ten thousand things.*

—Dao De Ching

*Late have I loved Thee, O Beauty ever ancient, ever*
*new, late have I loved Thee.*

—Augustine of Hippo

*The bhakti path winds in a delicate way.*

—Kabir

# Contents

# Homecoming

*Kabir says: Listen, my friend,*
*there is one thing in the world that satisfies,*
*and that is a meeting with the Guest.*
—Kabir

# *Lectio Divina*

With my mother's pitted paring knife
I slice the yellow, uncut pages.
*La Vida de Santa Teresa de Jesus.*
No tears. Then,
her voice.

Is it just the old story of wander
and homecoming that triggers this
in breath—Euricleia touching Odysseus's scar?

When I was young her words were gold
leaf, plucked strings, feathery. I trembled
at *Muero porque no muero!*
*I die because I do not die!*
in Him. I turn pages and her steel
flashes. *Descanso? I need no rest.*
*What I need is crosses.*

Or is it the way I've found my
dawn cries lifted, sung
by a woman, an Atlantic
away, centuries ago, in a convent
of barefoot nuns, a town of stone and light,
in a book I've called from a warehouse,

acids hurrying it to dust, pages
never cut open until now?

O, *Santa Teresa,*
may your words that I am breathing,
in this slow disappearing,
light my way to Avila.

# The Middle Way

*—for Jennifer*

I was entering the middle of the end of a divorce from a woman who'd appeared like the sun and the moon to me, and who, incredulous, was herself in the middle of an affair with a woman, and when confronted, locked herself in the bathroom and cut at her wrists.

I was exploiting a post-separation rebound affair with a tall blonde German in black leather whom I goaded into hurting me for all that I had done and not done.

I was in the middle of a five-year game of Hold'm, Low Hole Wild, Stud, and Fuck Your Buddy—joneses of triumph and rage—proxy catharses for the real crap I was in.

I was stitching together a book out of elder, mullein, and pokeweed,

putting away icons of Jesus, Mary, Shiva, Sarasvati, converting to a bad Buddhism,

burning court briefs in the pit behind the house.

I was in the middle of therapy.

It was June in the house of my vacationing Calvinist professor. On the fourth floor of her Tudor mansion, gabled like an attic, though an attic hovered above, I climbed into her claw-foot tub,

and in hot water beside a wall of a hundred tiny window
panes cascading down to the porcelain, I gazed out through
handkerchief-waving poplars to an Ann Arbor street.

And somewhere in the middle of *Tropic of Cancer* and *The Life
of Teresa* I picked up the phone and the nerve and called and
asked you to canoe with me down the Huron River where around
a willowy bend, I promised, a great blue heron would lift itself
impossibly off the water,

not knowing that out of the mud and muck of the middle of things,
something was unfolding, being born,

that we would marry and raise sons in the West.

Sunlight cut through maples and oaks, dazzled water that cradled
me, and you said, *Yes*, and I lay my head back on the marble,
knowing I'd just been made king in a house and story I did not own.

# Eckhart says

as the leaves of a tree
        turn,
    a hart
        or a woman turns
    towards lightning before
        it strikes, we turn
    toward You.

Across the river, a voice calls, like
    a parent's, a lover's, a child's.
        The boatman pulls the boat onto the water.
    I climb in and watch as the bow is swept
        into the rainbow mist
    and thunder
of the Ganges River.

# What He Left

—*for my father*

1.

With a glass of Kentucky bourbon
lit by a lamp, I leaf my father's *Life
and Literature of England*,
eleven hundred pages, mid-century
woodcuts, broken spine, floated down
to me after his death. I track him to The Rose,
The Abbey, to nightingales in the lime-tree bower,
gathering words he left in the margins, minted
in his hand: *Chiasmus. Caesura. Learn by heart.*
His name like a mantra in Kentucky hieroglyphs:
*Walter. Walter. Walter.*
I feel the sultry summer classroom,
nineteen fifty-four, felt trousers,
fan whirling, mockingbird trills.

2.

September. Seventy-five. Under yellow poplars
Doctor Haddin stood up in the grass, and said,
*Why, I've read Walden like it was the only book
in the world.* With black beard and blowing hair
he took out his violin to prove it. He was
Chagall's green fiddler, leapt
down from the English balcony,
flinging cardinals, goldfinch, indigo buntings, out of
Bach's *Chaconne in D*, and I knew I'd found my home.

3.

On two-twenty-seven, my mother's name
    dangles like an ornament
        between the columns
    of the "Eve of Saint Agnes."
        *Kathleen*
        *Agnes*
        *Wall*
etched in the meticulous, drunken ink
of a cut heart. How much he made
of the *w*'s of their names!

    *W*'s flock and scatter,
              kettle,
         and cascade,
  wingtips
      linked through
  a hundred years of poetry.

4.

Later that year, armed with newer metrics, he flew
to the Philippines to tap out code to
brigades in Korea, and came home wounded
to scale the towers of a dying industry—red-faced
at traffic, at bosses younger than him, at splintered
trusses, broken deals and bikes and sons breaking away.

5.

Once, his face candled by firelight,
he loosed the galloping dactyls, six hundred

in suicidal charge of the Light Brigade.

6.

Kentucky whiskey warms my chest, but I'm
late for the lesson—the story of a boy
who one summer, in love with my mother,
learned poems by heart and left words
in the margins I would never hear him say.

*Terza Rima. Heroic couplet. Alexandrine.*

# After Byodo-In

Candlelight, blue wreaths
of smoke encircle the cypress
Buddha brought back from Byodo-In,
Valley of the Temples, Oahu.

I settle into my breathing, returning
to this practice after years away, years
chasing mirages, veils, moon rivers.

The golden Buddha of the temple
on his thousand-petaled lotus
floats before my mind. My love and I

flew to this bracelet of islands,
where she played among plumeria
bougainvillea, and palms. And on Na Pali
cliffs above the wrinkled water,
I saw how love demands a remaking.

Years away from this tower,
this templum, I wait
for signal fires, the first
cracks in the carapace of self.

# Wednesday Morning, Pocatello, Idaho

*—for Ford and Susan Swetnam*

1.

I wake to canted light, a friend's mountain
fastness, the sun's first oils already dry,
my love beside me,
my friend in Florence, looking at all
that love and cancer will allow.

Now that the world has emptied
the neighborhood, a clock counts minutes of light.
Purple irises rise from cut glass as if
about to sing. Ford's books stand
in their cases, goldfinch at his feeders,
a child's voice lifts from the street.

This is the ore the scholars are after,
cloistered in the libraries of the world,
under painted ceilings,
a yellow pencil whispering to
its shadow in slow turns across the page,

what the backyard mechanic is trying to repair
out at night under the engine,
solving little problems, sliding the washer
onto its shaft, whirling the nut into place,

what we watch for in embers outside the tent,
or behind the green curtain
above the canoe where Orion
wades into the water.

When my love awakes, she puts on a robe,
sips coffee by the window, light
pouring in like milk from a pitcher,
a clink of the cup on the saucer.

## 2.

And I am five again, my father
at work, brother Joe at school,
Nancy in her crib, my mother
sewing or writing a letter.
I'm lying in bed, looking out the window.
Joy, gold-winged, flutters to the eaves.
I get up, put on my clothes,
and know without knowing
that something is calling me
out of this silence.
I try not to make a sound

# Often I Pray

at four in the morning quietly
moaning, trying not to wake my wife.
For ten years I have wept. Ancient
oil pours out.
Chogyam Trungpa Rinpoche says, *At the heart
of existence is sadness.* But he drank too much.
Votive candles, painted statues, incense
bring no solace.

Yet, what am I beside the fathers
    of Palestine, Israel, Darfur?
How much sleep have they been getting?
Does the afterburn of their childhood
wounds fan the cries of their children?

Krishna said to Arjuna,
    *Meet me on the battlefield.*
A friend says,
    *What is meditation?*
I say,
    *A garden for tears.*

# Hiking Entrada,
# Aidan Not Yet Born

Bridge Canyon. February slickrock.
Dry fork, Dolores
River. Clouds dark, pregnant.
New snow silhouettes sage and junipers,
pinyon pine, stipples the face
of canyon cliffs.

Yesterday we spun wheels towards
this hideout and
backtracked to Moab for chains.

Prickly pear, petroglyphs, animal bones.
A raven arrows off the cliff—
a chip of obsidian
off Entrada ochre.

*It's our last trip before children,* I think.

Though already we're four
curled on a canyon floor
out of the February wind:
you're spooned in the crook
of my body, Aidan curled in yours,
Pippin, the border collie,
circled before him.

Staying warm's the work.

*Quoark,* say the ravens.
    *A raucous caucus,* I observe.
        But you're not paying attention,
plying the oars of sleep.

*One body,* says our breath,
    as the shutter of the world opens,
        and light streams out of the clouds.

# *Maya,* Freak Show

The gastroenterologist will later say
it was a bug from Machu Picchu.
But tonight they're trying a pic line—fine tube
a nurse will slide into a vein of my arm, wriggle up
and over my shoulder, where it can burrow down
to hover over the superior vena cava of the heart.

Laid up for three days, yesterday they forced
a vacuum hose up my nose and down
my throat (it's the about-
face that makes you yell out) to my gut to pump
my small intestine, since a goblin
called the ileum clenched his fist,
and I doubled over, going
down in a David-Lynch carnival of pain.

My love's brought music—not what I hope
she'll play the hour I exit the world—
Beethoven, Tchaikovsky's Fifth,
*Concierto de Aranjuez*—
but Rumi, kirtan, ragas, Kabir.

White-coated seraphim flit about,
granting wishes for kindness
and Demerol, more than prescribed. I see
my mother. She's twenty, in her white
nurse's cap. Krishna Das sings to Ma Kali,

Durga, *Jagatambe*, Mother, Lover,
Destroyer.

Jennifer holds my hand and our unborn Aidan,
as the nurse makes the cut and threads
the pic line in.

# Something Keeps Fixing Things

missteps, miseries, misanthropies,
cowerings and cringings in sage and cheat
grass. I turn around, turn back, turn
coat. Pale. Err. Cling to fear's frigate.

And free will? I think of that famous friggin'
at the Edenspot. O, *Felix culpa,* Mendelssohn
and cat. My errors line up, lie down
along the snake. Kundalini, tattooed one,
thy poison hath become my medicine.

And the middle way ain't straight. It turns
through switchbacks, alleyways,
bawlings, brawlings, boudoirs
and barroom stenches.

So, turn around like Lot's wife.
See, the old camel's zigzag
wending its way across the sand,
a constellation plotted
long ago on a map in the lap
of Zarathustra.

# Old Faithful Inn, Yellowstone

## 1.

A red-eyed towhee sings in the prairie grass.
Marsh Creek under a bronze October
gong. A cool breeze flutters aspen flags.
Goateed Justice Jordan removes his hat and lays down
a path of words to our future. We stand
above the elk wintering grounds,
Jackson Hole, Wyoming, and I'm crying
more than you. Middle-aged strangers
and violet Tetons bear witness.

Aidan, new moon inside you,
hears it all.

## 2.

Then, purple grapes, clusters of dates, olives,
Camembert, Shiraz, and cake make dinner
on an atrium balcony of Old Faithful Inn, where
trunks and limbs lift a forest of balconies.
You point to the distant ceiling where
a window frames stars, another crescent.
I uncork champagne, you slice the cake.
A piano plays Ravel, Chopin bells.

3.

Toward midnight we walk among white dragons
    unfurling from geyser cauldrons,
hear bull elk bugle along
    the Madison, under the Starry River.
*All my life*, I say,
    *I wanted to live in the West.*

You, in my arms, say, *Listen.*
    *Coyotes, yipping*
        *at the honeymoon.*

# Into darkness

I

plummet
weightless
God of Abraham God of Isaac
I cannot
breathe
blind
velocites
naked broken
something
seizes seizes
and I am
soaring
talons
clutching me
in the down
of some wildly
beating
breast

# In the Garden

Jennifer works in her study. Dinner and dishes done. I'm out in the backyard, in early-summer air, putting in a garden above the barn—basil, rosemary, cardamom, sage. Saffron alpenglow on the ridges of the east. Krishna, new puppy with one blue eye, is helping out. (In a few months, she'll wander over snow down to the highway, looking for us.) She digs the black dirt, sticks her nose in, snorts, leaps back, barks, and plunges in again. I've turned over the ground on the eastern slope, taken the grass out, built terraces, and brought stones from the creek to shore things up. Now I'm breaking clods with my hands. Cool dirt, soft, crumbly. Krishna snores in the dusk under an apple. From a fence post, a meadowlark drenches the air. I stand up and reach for some blue-winged swallowtail of childhood.

# My Beloved's Eyes

When You first came to me,
    and I looked into Your eyes,
        I died,
    as Moses warned,
        and did not die. I
wept.

As the sun pulls the apple blossom
    inside out,
        Your eyes drew
           me.

I became Whitman's
    spider, Kabir's dolphin,
        Augustine's circle.

The fact that Your eyes are dark
    with the dust of galaxies
        wholly undoes me,

and I see that that undoing
    is what we long for and turn
        from in anyone's eyes—

as on that hungover morning
    walking the streets of Atlanta,
        looking for Garcia Lorca,
           when I caught the blues of an army vet
           with a Colt .45
           on the fire escape steps.

# Receiving *Jukai*

Last night my buddy Jake was initiated
at the Big Money Zen Center
in a room smoked with sandalwood
and candles, bells, gongs, and priests in robes.
The works. Ad copy says Big Money's
connections go right back to the Buddha.
Home of the Five-Five-Fifty— famous meditation retreat
where five aspirants for five days receive
hands-on ministrations from the Big Roshi, himself,
for "a significant donation" of fifty thousand dollars.
I'm not kidding.

I myself fell in with a cult of fools,
god-drunk poets, madwomen,
and snake haired prophetesses.
The lineage is as crooked as lightning.
Transmission of the dharma passes
outside of the scriptures, through winks and nods,
and our avatars sprout like weeds around the porch.

Our founder sits in meditation under the oak leaf
at my foot. Our stupas line streets like telephone poles,
and our temples are roadside tables, lonely
precipices, Walmart cafes, and greasy corner grills.

Big Money's scriptures are housed in vaults,
ours secreted under the blackbird's wing,

in droplets hanging at the eaves of your house.
Our temple roofs arc with unhewn pine
and our floors are covered in straw.

One noble truth says,
    *All things are singing*
*(inside you).*

One sutra says,
    *The Shiraz of love makes everyone*
*burst out laughing.*

So, relax the knitted brow
    and down-turned mouth, put up
        the rulebook, judgment stick,
            canon and beads.

    Then, the Holy One will take up His flute
        and play love songs for you
            in that chamber of the heart-temple
            we closed the door on
        so long ago.

# Leaving Home

When I saw in the *Herald Journal* that my Beloved
was coming to town, I poured coffee
all over the eggs.

Now I'm on my knees in the closet, throwing out clothes,
suits, ties, jeans and sweaters,
Hendrix albums, Sex Pistols tapes,
Social D CDs, stereo and tape deck,
classic novels, unread poetry, textbooks, law books,
*Life, The New York Review of Books,* love letters
from the IRS, hate mail, junk mail, pornography.
In the garage, I toss spare parts, spare tools, jars
of nails and screws. I've got to vacuum the van,
change the oil, flush the radiator.
And the weeds in the backyard, the fucking weeds!
And the roof! The god-damned roof!
Kick out dog and cats, the whole family.
Everybody out! Cut the lights. Go out
into the empty streets.
We'll take the train, the Via Negativa, get away,
not speak, not move, not breathe.

But there on the platform, the smoke clears,
and we've missed the train. An orange monk under
a lavender oleander with a macaque
on his back winks: *You have to leave home
to make a start.* But wait, I say.
Can't we talk this over?

He flips a rupee coin and says, *Try this:*
*Empty the other house. The Woman*
*who's been coming to you in dreams*
*has been waiting to give birth*
*to Herself inside you.*

# Aidan Looks at the Moon

After the bugling of elk,
dinner by the wood stove,
we turned in, slept until midnight,
and then you woke crying, inconsolable. I
carried you out of the cabin,
across the porch, where September
poured over us
with fragrance of sage
and you were hushed.

In the moon-lacquered dark
aspens quaked with owls,
and I looked at you
awake in my arms,
five-months old,
eyes like pearls
staring at the moon—
that lantern lighting
this field and continent—

your first time to look at
the famous orb
that lit the plains of Troy,
the face implored by Sappho and Sidney,
that Li Po leapt for, drunk
and drowning, crone of Whitman,
Hecate to Plath.
O Ariel, O huntress,

light this boy's nights
when he hikes these mountains
or comes home late from cards
or loving, illuminate his honeymoon
and housewarming,
and when he grows past
all my wanderings,
soften his sleepless nights,
as you have mine,

when I walk the house
in the dark
and find you in a window,
reminding me again that beyond
whatever carapace
of longing or fear
I've wrapped around myself,
something calls to me
from a home where the elk
steps in the river.

# When God wakes up
# inside you

you'll lift your head like a sun-
    flower in a field where the drops
        of dew have risen to the tips
of every blade of grass. You'll be
    that bead of iridescence
        ready to be taken up in the air.

On the day God turns to you
    those dark forest eyes,
        you'll find yourself in a theater
watching an opera of your life,
    standing up and yelling,
        *I thought it was a tragedy!*
        *I thought it was a tragedy!*

And when She comes from her bath
    perfumed and newly robed do you
        think you'll ever get that grin off your face?
    When Her robe falls to the floor
        (did I say *Hers*? Did I mean *His*?)
            *O dichosa ventura!*

The rest of the day, the rest of your life, you'll see
    those eyes everywhere,
        looking into the architectures

of light. Then only dancing
  will make sense,
    breathing Her breath,
      His, until you find yourself
      looking out the irises
        of every stranger's eyes.

# November, Hiking with Aidan, Seven Months Old

You chant koans and mantras
as we reach the canyon cliffs, high above
the Bear River, twisting its jade way, far below,
wrinkled and seamed with white.

You're startled by thunder, and soon we're in rain
and snow. I rig a raincoat shelter under a pine,
where the ground is littered with needles
and hoofprint hearts. I lift you out of your backpack
and settle you in my lap, as a raindrop
smacks you right between the eyes. *Tilak!*

Stinging hands hold a bottle
I kept warm inside my shirt,
and you drink your mother's milk.

What's this landscape to your seven-month eyes?
Face of a father, spiraling flakes,
silver needles, juniper perfume,
all nameless.

> When they pulled you
from your mother, you came into a wilderness.
Now, we're trying to show you how a home might be.
Gulping milk, you gaze in my eyes,
and I curl over you, blocking the snow,
the bottle a candle between us.

# *Keep prayer simple*

says the unknown author
  of *The Cloud of Unknowing*.

Distill it to a word, a syllable, like *love*
  or *God*. Repeat it
like the beat of the vulture's wing,
    waves on a Greek shore,
      the breath of the pulse.

But I say Your name once,
    my Swan, my Beloved,
and start to cry.

So many years apart—
    the two of us like
      a broken pomegranate.

Salt water of exile, water of
    homecoming, wet
      my hands.

Yes, Your eyes beckon,
    but who will steer the ferry
to carry me to the country
    where what is inside me
      can be born inside You?

# December, Hiking with Aidan, Eight Months Old

At fir line, four feet of snow,
north skies clearing to hyacinth,
a cloud-shrouded sun to the south, I stop.
Three ravens pass over. In prisms and juniper
berries, our border collie coils in black coat and
tail, staring up at me with acorn eyes.
My son sleeps in his backpack, wrapped
in quilted down. I stand the contraption
beside a snow-capped rock, his feet hanging
just above the white, his breath
moving like a trout in slow current
under ice. A chatter of chickadees.
I sip green tea in snowshoes. A white serpent
unfurls from the cup. I open Su Tung Po, pray
Aidan won't wake and cry.
*Just five minutes to stand and read*

of a cliff-hung monastery where monks
sit in silence, candles sputtering, smoke
of incense, meditation bells.
A dawn wind stirring.

There is a practice, a way,
in this fathering, but not much
*noble silence.* Instead, I attend to
fist-clenched panics and moon-mouthed

emergencies. I begin a twenty-year *sesshin*
and already I've found that
the Buddha in the backpack
has the koans to break my heart
open. Swirling from the canyon
comes a snow-sharpened wind.
I hoist the backpack and sleeping boy
and we are heading home.

# After Meditation

I open my eyes after an hour riding
a raft of breath to estuary waters.
Darkness guards the house.
My son and wife asleep, cats fed,
dog curled by my thigh,
a cup of tea in my hands, I read
the *Gospel of Ramakrishna.*

Outside the window stretches *my own private Idaho.*
White pillars, porch rails glowing
*as if they were alive,* and the rough trunks
of weeping spruces shoot up in silence.
In the valley, the first ranch lights coming on.
Sound of two creeks, song of a meadowlark,
three sisters vanish into dawn.

A poet I love is vanishing—
his body riding the rigging of his lines,
new timbers laid down every day.

When I hear the slippers of my beloved
my heart breaks like a lantern.
Dawn floods the house. Scarlet clouds, gilt-edged,
bloom from the horizon. Saltwater
on my lips. For thirty years I lived
in exile. Now, Ramakrishna
says what enlightenment is:
*A doll made of salt dives for the bottom of the ocean.*

# Hiking at Oselong, Tibetan Buddhist Monastery of Andalucía

1.

The white villages
of Bubion, Pampaneira, Capeleira
cling to cliffs like candle wax, while
poplars clang a thousand summer chimes.
Hermitages hide in grottos and crevices
under prayer flags fluttering wildly in the sun,
tongues proclaiming that we stand on a threshold.

Beyond the next peak, the sea at the center of the world.

Monasteries draw me, and I'm terrified of them.
Terrified of the call. That something in the rock will rivet
a needle inside me and I'll decide to stay. Buddha left
his family, like Mirabai, Indira Devi, Peter, and Paul.
I followed that call once, crushing
hearts like soda cans, but then came home.

2.

But you're not thinking about any of that, little one,
fifteen months old, riding my hip and smiling.
No one welcomed us at the office. The monks
are on retreat. On retreat from a monastery!
An ocean of silence laps everything,

wide as the sky, like the peal of a gong,
like the drone of the giant stupa spool at the gate.
*Om Mani Padme Hum. Jewel in the heart of the lotus.*

3.

We take a path across the cliff, above
clouds, gorge, and valleys. Your eyes
gazing into mine, smiling. Usually, they turn away
and you point to a tree, a cat. But today,
they're blue and gazing steadily.
I think you have a secret.

*Everything's shining,* I go on.
*Even the rocks!*
*It's like we're in the Home of the Immortals.*
*The Pure Land of the Bodhisattvas!*
*Abode of Avalokitesvara!*

And that's when I trip.

We pitch forward. A star
of fear bursts in my chest.
I shift you to the crook
of my arm. Squeeze you as we hit rock,
dirt. My right hand, knees,
can't stop us.
We somersault and land.
*God damn it!*
I yell into monastery silence.
I check, and you're okay. In fact,
you're still looking into my eyes.

In fact, you're laughing.
We sit in the dirt and laugh, as the Buddha
behind your eyes says: *Even in paradise,
you have to pay attention.*

I lie back and you sit on my belly,
say *dah-dah,* for *dog-dog,* point at my red
knees, at the prayer flags, the sky,
your mother coming up the trail.

True north everywhere.

# Shoveling Snow

Your book says this snow was poured out of the moon.
We're shoveling it, out before dawn.

In hand-me-down boots and dark blue mittens
you've finished the work with your broom

and stand there staring at me in ten-below wind,
which flattens the down of your coat.

I scrape and heave, scrape and heave,
making a berm beside the walk.

Pippin, our border collie, leaps,
hurls a ball in the air. The owl in our willow

hoots in the dawn. I talk as your cheeks redden,
your eyes clear and tearing, but you won't go in,

not until I do. Behind your breath, a smile.
What do I make of how you matched your broom

to my shovel, of this tether at the heart
and animal-belonging to each other?

*Let's go in,* I say and take your hand.
We turn toward the house, the solstice,

a few stars still out, day by day,
writing the history of your life.

# Fire Sermon

The world is burning, said Heraclitus
    and Buddha
and Jesus in his way,
    and before them—
        the rishis of the Vedas.

Aidan and I huddle outside the tent.
    Orange coals, yellow flames, sapphire,
hold our gaze. Across the horizon
    Draco flies.

*Hold out your hands. Feel how warm?*
    *Don't grab at the flames.*

The world is like this, too,
    though I don't say that.
        Love, with its own fire.

Simone Weil found the spark
    in the difference between
        *looking* and *eating*.

A sannyasi leaves home,
    puts on a saffron robe, becomes
        a walking flame.

# Housekeeping

And we are put on earth, a little space,
That we may learn to bear the beams of love.
—William Blake

What is the sense of leaving your house?
—Kabir

# Kellen in My Lap,
# Five Months Old

In a circle of lamplight I read again
Suzuki's *Zen Mind, Beginner's Mind.*

You play my fingers like piano keys, arranging
and rearranging them, finding

new patterns, melodies. When you woke
in the three o'clock dark

we moved out here to a room
where you could play and I could work.

*What is satori?* Suzuki asks. *The bottom of a pail
broken through.* Coyote, mountain lion

stalk the hills above our house. Darkness
holds its wing above the valley. Orion

brightens January snow and down in the far fields
flickers a single yellow windowpane.

The delight you find in my fingers
a monk has no words to name.

# Morning Song

C   Summer nights, we pulled fireflies
      from the dark, our hands became
      lanterns. A child's trick, sure.

C/A But on that morning when trees on
      the highest ridge catch fire,
  and behind the mountains inside you
A      the Holy One rises
      like sun on bronze,

C  you'll lie back in the grass
      among the drowsing fireflies,
A     as the falcon in the word
      of the poem takes off,

C  and you close your eyes to the cry
A    of one name echoing
      through canyons, creeks, and clouds.

# In the Face of It

After midnight
    you wake me again,
        second son,

not yet one,
    laughing
        in your sleep.

Abraham
    named his second *Isaac:*
        for *one who laughs.*

Your name's
    Gaelic,
        for *warrior.*

They took you up Mount Moriah
    the day you were born—
        Intermountain NICU—

bound and abraded you for days,
    with IVs, feeding tubes, ventilators, injections.
        White coats hurrying about with their terrible

ministrations. Tonight, I think you dream of the lowing
    in the cedars and the flash of a knife
        vanishing in the sky.

# Yesterday I saw
# Your heart open

like Mary's, crowned
in my *Child's*
    *Picture Book of Saints.*

Inside glittered constellations, galaxies,
    an ocean I saw I could enter
    in my little boat.

Now I've been floating
    in this place
        for a thousand years,

playing on my flute
    the songs You taught me
    in another life.

I've lost my coordinates,
    my map, my route, my ticket,
    my name, my number.

All my cares blown out
    with a whisper, like candles
    at a meadowlark's song.

# Kellen, First April

Steady in the new grass, feet spread
    wide like a lifter's,

you stand by your red dragon
    blanket, head thrown back and laughing.

In your right hand you wave a wand
    as your left reaches for cirrus.

I'm on my back reading Wilbur's "Praise
    in Summer." And metaphors

tumble out: You're Bernstein conducting
    "Finches in a Blue Spruce,"

the child Adam praising another day,
    Juwertamakai conjuring

buzzard and coyote, Brahma reborn,
    fingers spinning starry pinwheels,

baby Ajax lifting the pillars of heaven.
    But then the poet asks, "Why this mad *instead?*"

Can I not see you as you are *at all?*
    Eleven-month-old, sure-footed, second son,

transfixed by sunlight, the mystery
of balance, a finch-fringed tree.

*Power resides in the shooting of the gulf,*
said Emerson,

and like the *goddess of secret and ancient*
*coincidences,* Rilke named rhyme,

perhaps our leaping
passes our kenning.

Maybe you're not the tenor of my imaginings at all—
but the vehicle—having leapt

from your mother's body, half-fledged of me,
restringing lovers' genes,

and eyeing a future we will never see.
Now you shake your stick and yell

at the sky, while across the April grass
a thousands suns light up your feet.

# Ever since,

I can't stop wondering if I died.

I'd been nursing my favorite griefs
    like a baby or a drunk his bottle
when You came strolling in sandals
    down White Swan Lane to lay
        your hand upon my forehead.

I remember a brimming, and then
    the flood. Tulips in crystal toppled
over. Walls and windows fell
    away. I felt my skin dissolving,
pores, veins opening,
    a body become transparent,
spaces between atoms visible.
    I could hear Mirabai calling.

Then the world hushed, like dawn
    on the Bay of Bengal. Everything vanished
        in the quicksilver of morning.
    Far distances rested my eyes.

It was a lucky throw, a gold coin,
    a winning ticket,
        all grace and gladness,
    my ship come in with perfumed sails.
        And who was that singing at the helm?

Friend, I'll tell you a secret. That gold coin's
        in your pocket, the ticket's
            sewn in your sleeve.
        There's a ship at the wharf with your name
            on the hull and flying on the flag.

# The Fourth Noble Truth

*—for Kellen*

Early walker, one year old,
    you took off with a topo-map
        stolen from our open car door.

Laughing down the empty street,
    you thought you were the new
        Jesse James.

But then you tripped and, clutching your booty
    too tightly—map of Mt. Naomi, veined as any heart—
        you had no hands to spare,

and your face met the cement. Then, O,
    the blood, the tears,
        and holding.

It takes time, my son, to learn
    to break a fall by letting go
        of what you want.

# When You leave
# my house

in the night without a word,
and I don't know if You are ever coming back—
can't You understand what that's like?

You say I'm dramatic. But
remember Herzog's *Nosferatu,*
and the ghost ship that slides up the canal
of that Dutch village, breaking the branches
of the sycamores as it comes to a stop?

Who can say how it got there?
There's no one on board. No one
at the helm. Just a coffin
and a thousand starving rats
bringing the Black Death
to another sleepy town.

My house is that town.

# Checking Out

Kafkaesque, I walked through my house,
my marriage, past ungrateful sons fraying
my wits' last rope ends, holding me tenuously to cliffs
of rage. Exhausted, sleepless, sick of boys
fighting over toys that, like boys themselves,
won't shut up: *Push my button! Pull my string!*
*I'll never be your friend! Fine!*
*Take everything! Take it all!*
*I hate you to the ends of the universe!*
I sank into the ancient bile-well of hatred
of my life, myself, my chances,
until I'd had enough and just checked out.
Said goodbye to all that.

Not by the usual means—the .38
my mother's father used when I was four,
or the macho writer's double-barreled bonanza,
not by truck fumes, Plath gas, cyanide, Cicero bath,
Nic noose, frozen-Mississippi-River bridge-jump,
ex-wife's razors, or the rock star's autoerotic get-off.

No, not with the Remington my neighbor used up in the hills,
a father who left his son in his pickup while he scouted hunting spots
in the Wellsvilles, the two-year-old getting out, wandering off,
days later found frozen, the father sentenced, and doing it
in the slender days before incarceration.

And I didn't *go out for milk*—the trick of my parents' neighbor,
who gunned his pickup, his hot new starling

perched beside him on the seat,
wheels turned like a rifle toward Las Vegas.

True, one time, in a dead-end marriage, I rolled
my station wagon across I-40, Stravinsky blaring,
sparks streaming from the roof,
splinters of glass swirling like a Firebird
before my face when out of nowhere
came a question: *Are you ready?*
*Not yet.*

Still, nothing changed much,
until I learned one
more thing.

Who can say how it happened? I saw the way out
    the in-door. I became myself
    the car I totaled,
    the bullet chasing stars,
    flames wreathing the body,
    the bridge I leapt from,
    Mississippi water filling the lungs.

Somebody helped, it's true, as I stepped out
    into the sky, shouting
at God that he was nothing
    but an empty cipher
for something a billion suns
    brighter,
*tat tvam asi, tat tvam asi,*
which we
are.

# Pierre Teilhard de Chardin Cut-up

A flame has lit up the world
        within,        radiant word,
    lay hold of me, absorb me,
                it is you I desire,
torrent of fearful energy,
             I stretch out my hand,
O fiery bread,
        *Tu autem, Domine mi,* include me
           *in imis visceribus Cordis tui,*
                      purify,
set me on fire,
    your breast a furnace,

trails of phosphorescence,
             rainbow hues,
*so close to oneself,*

    fiery chariot, horses-in-a-whirlwind,
           now
        matter casts off its veil,
      O fountain of transcendent / inexorable fixity,
influx of power
        *the whole universe aflame,*
      unalloyed delight,
   aureole thrilling and inundating,
my need for plenitude of being,

                              more me than myself
          objects lost,
    the more we lose a foothold in darkness the more deeply we
              penetrate into God,
    (splendor of all flowers,)
                         we have cause to tremble.

# The Doe

Mouths gleaming with diamonds, the Dobermans
in the pickup lunge at Aidan, Kellen, and me
as we get our daypacks out of the car.

When we've reached the canyon's ridge we turn
and see them crisscrossing through the sage,
zigzagging toward us, lithe as leopards,
tearing up the dust. A woman's yelling,
but she's not in control.

They angle closer, and Aidan says, *Daddy?*
*They won't bother us,* I promise,
but I pick them up. The woman yells
and they veer out of sight.

Under a scarred and twisted juniper
we share apricots, raisins, and cheese,
Kellen nestled between my legs.
Below us, two vultures, wings almost touching,
sail into the canyon like black surf.

*Daddy, what's that?* Aidan asks.
I turn and see it—a cluster of bones, ribs sticking up
like pick-up sticks, hide torn open,
a half-naked skull wrenched backwards,
staring at the catastrophe of its body.
*It's dead,* I say. Then Kellen:
*What does "dead" mean?*
I swallow. *Well, when your body*

*can't keep going anymore it just stops.*
*Stops?*
*Well,* I say, thinking fast,
*the part inside, the part that feels and thinks,*
*that part goes back up to the stars.*

They look up. The sun is reeling its broken red
light behind the Wasatch Mountains.

*Do people die?* Kellen asks.
*When they get old.*
*Are you old?*

I'm saved by the Dobermans charging
toward us like a fire. I pick up rocks, hurl
them, swoop the boys up.
The dogs swerve, tear down the slope.
At the gravel, they leap into the bed,
and the truck sputters off
dragging its long brown tongue of dust.

We stand a moment, feeling the warmth
between our bodies, hooked in patterns of holding,
three and five years old. I want to keep them here—behind
these crossed arms, in a world where cougars
leap smilingly through brightly painted books.

But we pick our way down the talus-strewn slope,
and they keep looking back toward the doe,
hungry for knowing, knowing I haven't
told all. The white bones like teeth
in the mouth of the canyon.

# Note to Self

Only by going up the stairs and disappearing into the attic,
or stealing that Mazda you've been eyeing at Discount Motors

and heading West toward absolute drunkenness,
tossing your books to the homeless,

adopting a life of listlessness,
the bed unmade, spaghetti dishes in the sink,

surrendering to Ma Kali as she draws the rake of sorrow across
your chest, soaking your self in purple dyes of dissolution,

dropping it all into the abyss,
I say,

only by crawling across the floor
and laying your head in Her lap,

gazing up through tears into those eyes of fire,
ignoring the galaxies spinning like tops across the floor,

will you ever learn to honor your family,
say you're sorry to the ones you've hurt,

satisfy banker and bankruptcy judge,
agents of collection and offended neighbors,

refit the pipes and broken fence,
yank bineweed, thistle, mallow, nettle.

No monastery can help you now—Soto,
Cistercian, Shaivite.

Too late for that.
You burned the bridges of religion.

Only when you take the job of janitor, your name
scrawled in an unknown tongue above the door

of a room in Her temple of the dawn
will you ever redeem your forfeit life.

# Meadowlark

1.

Halfway through September, I'm throwing
sticks for Pippin, and a meadowlark on a post
starts up his song. Days since I've heard one—
our yellow-breasted solitary, whose every phrase
says *spring*. Whitman would have called it
an aria. Maybe the last of the year.

I remember years ago when I listened to one.
We had quarreled, my wife and I, and I,
Otello—myself my own Iago—
stormed out of the house and into the truck
gunning it north for miles, past
sage-covered plains, the Bear River Massacre
Site, to Red Rock Pass, a sun-struck, red-butte
place, where fourteen thousand years ago
the Bonneville Sea burst its dam, spilling north
for hundreds of miles. Wagnerian.

There, on a broken cliff,
under Oxford Peak
I sat by a juniper in April sun,
while the ground burst
with avalanche lilies, and I listened.

2.

Now, my boys come running from their fort
of sage and big-tooth maples.
*Let me throw! I want a turn!*

I hand over the stick and smile that I can't now recall
the fight that day—the crescendo of voices
and infestations of hurt, the whole libretto and score.

But I remember the lilies and the singing
and light falling everywhere for miles—
how the smallest things around us become portals,
exits out of our darkened theaters
into the brightness of the afternoon.

# Delicate

1.

That morning Aidan's blue eyes were gazing into mine
    as he gulped his mother's milk
        I'd warmed in a bottle
    in a pan on the stove.
Outside, in the dark, Jennifer ran the white roads.

I rubbed the nipple across his lip so
    he'd take more, distracted by snow falling
outside the window, his eyes
    in a wordless watching
        beyond my reach. This white thread

is his tie to the world's provision,
    its offerings. But, no, not the world's—
        his mother's and mine.
Bone, muscle, tissue, tears, strung on this one thread.

And does it ever provide—the world, I mean—
    or must we always take?

2.

Across the field,
    the snow seemed and
        didn't seem like a bounty—
water for an arid valley, sure,
        but that first shower of falling stars—
    just weightless architecture.

We studied it in the dawn light,
   flakes falling,
      each in its own track.
The closest seem to fall faster
   while the far flakes more slowly
      all raining down
      at different velocities, graduated
         from here to there, a spectacle as
for our pleasure.

Unconvinced by arguments by design,
   I considered an argument from beauty.
Aesthetics everywhere—but yesterday,
      this same storm blew
      my friend's brother's semi
         right off the highway.

3.

A knock came from the back door
   and I lay Aidan on the sofa.
The mouth of a white-shirted stranger was saying,
   *Your wife. She's lying by the road.*
I grabbed my coat, boots, keys,
   spun wheels down the drive,
      then hurried back, lifted Aidan
      off the sofa, carried him gingerly over the ice,
shielding his face, and buckled him in.

4.

Jennifer loathes the winters here on the Idaho-Utah border.
   Once a jade and turquoise island

welcomed her to runs on paths
along the coast,
Jasmine, plumeria
blooming in winter.
Now a mile above the Pacific, winter
provides below-zero mornings,
with no help from the wind.

5.

*Like a deer*, I thought,
the fawn we came upon in Michigan
crying in ferns by the trail.
Spotted, tiny, crying out.
To us?
To the world?

6.

Jennifer lay shivering in the snow,
her limbs thin and folded
the way I folded mine around her
our first night by the Huron River,
grass wet, no blanket, and recited
the one about the red bird:
*faith arranged in filamented principles
moving from pink to crimson at the final quill.*

I stroked her forehead,
EMTs brought more blankets.
I got Aidan from the car.
Fallen on the ice, she'd seen the van
skidding down hill behind her

and thought, *I have to get up,*
*for Aidan.* Hit while rising,
knocked off the road.
(Emergency will say nothing's
broken, but her runs will hurt for years.)

7.

This morning, in the dark on the sofa,
Aidan and Kellen, five and three,
drink milk and honey from sippy cups. We trace
car shadows across the walls,
talk pterodactyl dreams,
and wait for her return
to the fire we've made.

Outside the window, a doe and her fawns
stop on their way to the mountains,
having seen what the suburbs have to offer—
all our red tulips.

Our boys' voices, the warmth
of our bodies, a house finch's song, Jennifer
opening the door, her beauty,
fragility, all held lightly, none of it
ours, cared for, vanishing.

# I Said to the Beloved, *Are You Real*?

When You first came to me, pouring oils
    over my body like sunlit water, I kept asking:
        *Are you real? Are you real?*

Or some Freudian ghost, faking these ecstatic,
    *oceanic feelings,*
        like orgasms—vestiges of infantile

narcissism, or something. Well, You've been entertaining me a
    while now,
    and I'm beginning to think that not only
        are You not a phantom,

figment, siren, or banshee,
    but may be in fact more real
        than Coca-Cola, McCoys,

and the macaws down at the zoo.
    And then it occurs to me that not only are You
        *the real thing,*
            but You may be the *only real thing.*

This wide, wide, phenomenal world,
    I think is what hangs like a moving curtain
        in the balance, loose, by a thread.
See it shimmer, vanishing

before our eyes. I think that's what needs
    a little scaffolding, a little

mending, a little shoring up.

I'm just a monkey child
   clinging to your back
      as you cast the spell of
         another spectacular world.

# Handing Down Apple Branches

I'm up in the gnarled apple, thinning branches, trying for
a better yield. Orioles, goldfinch flit at the feeders.
Below, my sons ply their saws and clippers.

One rasping laugh at a time, my grandfather's bow saw
slices the wood. *Let the saw do the work,* I hear him say.
Sunlit sawdust rains on my boys.

And what was it my father said that spring day under the apples
of the monastery, where I'd stopped on my way to India
and monastic vows? Something about a woman in Charleston,

South Carolina, who asked me not to go. I hand the branches down.
Aidan and Kellen stack them. I showed them how to use their tools.
*Watch your fingers. Draw it easy. Let the saw do the work.*

Now my father, grandfather, and blue-eyed
Charlestonian come to me only in dreams.
Winter was long. My love, at the back door, calls.

We're glad for the sunlight, the orioles, and prisms
flashing at the eaves. *Come on, rascals. Dinnertime.*
Three and five, they still think I have the answers

and all the tools they'll need.

# When I First Pulled
# Onto the Highway of Love

*—after a line of Mirabai's*

When I first pulled onto the highway of love
all those years ago, no one told me
I couldn't ever get off.
Or perhaps someone did, but
when does a lover ever listen to talk like that?

I tried. There was the rollover when my Subaru
flipped on the median. Windshield splinters
choreographed in slow motion.
But it seemed I had more lives to live.
And there was the time I got off on an access road
that just wound right back onto an entrance.
How could I have known, Beloved Comedienne,
that all the roads were Yours?

That every exit, billboards for the Mandalay, Bellagio,
Four Seasons, and Ritz, with heated pools
and tropical gardens, personal attendants,
runways of delicacies, and a Khufu Pyramid ice bar
*With Over 100 Varieties of Vodka*, had all been arranged
by Your hand like a child's train set.

And anyway after so many twenty-four hour, all-you-can-eat
extravaganzas, with Vegas performers, high-wire
hookers, and then surfing the cable through the wee hours

from a Jacuzzi in another slate-and-marble bathroom—
I just climb back into the pickup
and hit the road.

Besides, ever since that dream when You
placed that prasad on my tongue, nothing else
tastes good anymore. I filled up at the Last-Gas
Exxon, got back in, and there You were,
riding shotgun, looking at the map.

Now I don't give a fig where we're going.
All Your sweet talk about Paradise, California,
and the cities of the Celestial Empire
is interesting, all right.
I just forgot how much I love to drive!

This highway's raven straight, and there's no one on it but us.
Saffron alpenglow lights the white sierras,
and I switch on the radio and cruise control
and You give me that sidelong glance, slide
over, and lay Your perfumed head on my shoulder.

# Dinner and a Movie, Green Canyon, Utah

As in a landscape painting of the T'ang,
snow silhouettes these black-and-yellow cliffs.
Subalpine fir stand green against the white,
holding fast for a spring that won't come.

Snow silhouettes the yellow limestone cliffs
though we can barely see any of it,
waiting for a spring that won't come
nestled in the back of our new minivan.

We watch the lights of Logan shimmer below
from the gravelly mouth of Green Canyon,
nestled in back of our new minivan
like lovers on that hill above Hollywood

above the California canyons.
And, in fact, we're watching a movie, *Juno*.
It's not Hollywood's take on Hera, wounded,
jealous, and roughing up old Hercules,

or is it? It's all about love, and we're eating tarts,
chocolate-filled, gifts of Mayan gods
(whom sanguine Mel offered up on film),
sipping oolong with night-blooming jasmine.

*Take this Mayan gift, this chocolate tart, my*
*tea cake, and I'll sing Happy Birthday!*

*We'll sip hot oolong with night-blooming jasmine,*
*for it's April, when faces called flowers float—*

*my little tea cake, Happy Birthday!*
For after a dinner at Le Nonne
(where flowers floated out of pots)
with *amatriciana, pomodora,*

a birthday dinner at Le Nonne,
with a nice Chianti and no dessert
(too much *amatriciana, pomodora),*
rather than steal into our home like thieves

tipsy with Chianti and no dessert,
and tiptoe down halls (*bye-bye,* to the sitter),
to watch a film without waking boys, like thieves,
we drove out here where beside our Sienna

a doe and three fawns step through sage
(*artemesia tridentada*),
like nymphs outside the car. Then, away
they leap, startled by headlights on a hill,

no one seeing Artemis draw her bow.
I worry it's the cops. You say, *We're legal!*
as snake eyes slowly slide down the hill.
*It's just kids—anxious for each other's tongues.*

But I worry, even if we're legal,
remembering high school nights in gravel lots,
teenage *joie de tongue* interrupted
by flashlights of the Alabama law.

The low-rider passes, and I sing
*Happy birthday, my bow-and-arrow beauty!*
*What flash or light of law or shooting star*
*could have called the hand that brought us here,*

*my bow-and-arrow beauty? Happy Birthday!*
Among these deer and stars not even Juno
could have called the hand that brought us here,
as into a film scene you'd wished you could be in,

with deer and stars, Juno and Artemis,
and subalpine fir standing green in the snow,
a canyon romance you've found yourself in
like a landscape painting of the T'ang.

# After the Sun

After the sun goes out,
    and earth, that blue-green pearl,
        breaks apart,

I'll be out there looking for You.
    And when I rest my head
        among the jade and purple petals

of your sari,
    breathing an air
        like the roses of Andalucía,

one white blossom,
    broken from its stem,
        will float

the river of my heart, anchor
    in that chambered cove
        where I first found You.

Then we'll laugh, leaning back, watching
    the little universes
        come and go,

and I'll dip my cup in your starry bowl,
    where Hamsa—the Swan—
        sings in the night sky.

# Acknowledgments

My thanks to the editors of these magazines who published the following poems, sometimes in slightly different forms.

*Five Points:* "First April," "Your Eyes"
*Pilgrimage:* "Checking Out," "After the Sun"
*Poetry Kanto* (Kyoto, Japan): "Aidan Looks at the Moon," "December, Hiking with Aidan, Eight Months Old," "Kellen in My Lap," "After Meditation," "Morning Song," "The Doe," "When God wakes up inside you"
*Post Road:* "Dinner and a Movie, Green Canyon, Utah"
*Sugar House Review:* "When You leave my house," "Fire Sermon," "Something Keeps Fixing Things"
*Wasatch Journal:* "November, Hiking with Aidan, Seven Months Old"

Deep gratitude goes to Nancy Rediger, my indefatigable and gracious editor at Truman State University Press; Jim Barnes, TSUP poetry editor; Barbara Smith-Mandell, my copy editor; and Diane Wakoski, who chose *The Empty Boat* for the 2004 T. S. Eliot Prize. I'd also like to thank the following, who read and commented on the manuscript or otherwise helped it come into being: David Bottoms, Ted Haddin, and Jim Mersmann, for long mentoring; Katharine Coles, for inspiration and poetic friendship; Mike Carson, for poetic and spiritual counsel; Jon Hershey, for Cloudland poetry and whiskey; Andrew Sofer, for careful criticism and true friendship; Ford Swetnam, for showing me ways to be a poet; Chris Cokinos, for poetry and wilderness comradeship, along with the other members of Splinters, my writing group, who helped with almost every poem: Ken Brewer, Jennifer Sinor, Kathe Lison, Charles Waugh, and Maria Melendez; also Anne Shifrer and Shawn Bliss; Anne Brown, for courage and love; Virginia Carstarphen, for love and underserved kindness; to my mother and late father, Kathleen and Walter Sowder, my aunt Eileen, sister Nancy, and brother Joe. I offer undying devotion to my spiritual teacher and guru, Ma Indira Devi, and to my dear friends at her ashram in Pune, India: Karishma and Udo Knipper and their son Sanju, and Rajkumar, Bharati, Manjula, Meenakshi, Kamlaji, Shumesh, and Shankarji. Finally, my deepest love and thanks go to my sweet boys, Aidan and Kellen, and my greatest love and partner, Jennifer Sinor.

# Notes

"Inscriptions"

*Bhakti*: Mentioned in the *Bhagavad Gita* (200 BCE–200 CE) as
the finest of the paths of yoga, *bhakti* is a spiritual path char-
acterized by ecstatic love for and devotion to the Divine, find-
ing expression in singing, dancing, art, and poetry. In fifth-
and sixth-century South India, a popular, anti-authoritarian,
anti-caste, *bhakti* movement was born and spread throughout
the subcontinent.

"*Lectio Divina*"

*Lectio Divina*: A Christian, especially monastic, practice of
spiritual reading, meditation, and prayer intended to pro-
mote communion with God.

"The Middle Way"

*The Middle Way*: The path to enlightenment taught by the
Buddha that navigates between the extremes of asceticism
and indulgence.

*Shiva*: The Hindu God of Destruction, though in Shaivism,
Shiva is considered to be the Absolute Reality and Divinity.

*Sarasvati*: The Hindu Goddess of Education, Art, Music.

"Eckhart Says"

*Meister Eckhart* (ca. 1260–ca. 1327): A German mystic and
theologian, excommunicated by the Catholic Church for his
teachings.

"*Maya,* Freak Show"

*Maya*: A tenet of many forms of Indian religion asserting
that the phenomenal world we experience is an "illusion," a
projection of ourselves, and that behind this veil of illusion is
Brahman, God, the only Real.

"Something Keeps Fixing Things"
*Kundalini*: In tantric and yogic systems, kundalini refers to a latent, female, spiritual power located in the base of the spine, coiled like a serpent, waiting to be awoken by spiritual practice.

"My Beloved's Eyes"
*Augustine's circle*: Augustine of Hippo (354–430) described God as a circle whose center is everywhere and whose circumference is nowhere.

"Receiving *Jukai*"
*Jukai*: A public ordination ceremony of initiation in Zen Buddhism.
*Roshi*: "Priest" in Zen Buddhism.

"November, Hiking With Aidan, Seven Months Old"
*Tilak*: A mark worn on the forehead by many Hindus, symbolizing the third eye, or sixth chakra, associated with meditation and spiritual enlightenment.

"After Meditation"
*The Gospel of Ramakrishna*: English version of a Bengali text that records conversations of Ramakrishna and his disciples. Ramakrishna (1836–86) was an Indian mystic and *bhakti* guru.

"Hiking At Oselong, Tibetan Buddhist Monastery Of Andalucía"
*Mirabai* (1498–1547): An Indian princess of Rajasthan who renounced her aristocratic life to become an ecstatic, penniless, wandering devotee of Krishna. Some 1,200 to 1,300 songs and poems attributed to her remain popular in India.
*Avalokitesvara*: One of the most revered bodhisattvas, who embodies the compassion of the Buddhas. Bodhisattvas are humans who have attained enlightenment but who have chosen to reincarnate to work for the enlightenment of all sentient beings.

"Kellen In My Lap, Five Months Old"
   *Satori*: A Japanese Buddhist term for enlightenment.

"In The Face Of It"
   *Mount Moriah*: The mountain that Abraham climbed to
   sacrifice his son, Isaac (Genesis 22:2). Also where Solomon
   began building the House of the Lord and where the Lord
   had appeared to David (2 Chronicles 3:1).

"Kellen, First April"
   *Wilbur*: Richard Wilbur, contemporary American poet, au-
   thor of "Praise in Summer."

"Ever since,"
   *Sewn in your sleeve*: Blaise Pascal wrote an account of a
   religious experience that begins: "The year of grace 1654,
   Monday, 23 November, day of St. Clement, Pope and Martyr.
   From about half past ten in the evening until about half past
   twelve, midnight, FIRE. God of Abraham, God of Isaac, God
   of Jacob. Not of the philosophers nor of the Wise. Assurance,
   joy, assurance, feeling, joy, peace. God of Jesus Christ." At his
   death, the account was found sewn into his sleeve.

"The Fourth Noble Truth"
   *The Four Noble Truths* of Buddhism comprise the acknowl-
   edgement (1) that human life is characterized by suffering,
   (2) that suffering is caused by craving and attachment, (3)
   that suffering can be overcome, and (4) that there is a path to
   overcome suffering.

"Checking Out"
   *Tat tvam asi*: Sanskrit mantra, translated as "Thou art That,"
   which indicates the oneness of the individual with the Divine.

"Delicate"
   *faith arranged . . . / . . . the final quill*: Lines quoted from Pat-
   tianne Rogers's poem, "Suppose Your Father Was a Redbird."

"When I First Pulled onto the Highway of Love"
   *Prasad*: Food offered to a deity or one's guru, which is then
   consumed by the devotee or disciple as consecrated.

"After the Sun"
   *Hamsa*: Sanskrit for "swan," a constellation in the night sky.
   *Hamsa* in Indian spiritualty came to mean purity, detach-
   ment, divine knowledge, cosmic breath, and spiritual enlight-
   enment. By separating the word's two vowels, it translates
   as "I am That" or "I am He," and is thus taken to signify the
   individual's union with the Divine.

# About the Author

Michael Sowder is a poet, writer, and professor at Utah State University in Logan, Utah, where he lives at the foot of the Bear River Mountains with his wife, writer Jennifer Sinor, and their two boys, Aidan and Kellen. His first book of poetry, *The Empty Boat*, won the 2004 T. S. Eliot Award and his chapbook, *A Calendar of Crows*, won the New Michigan Press Award. His nonfiction, which explores themes of wilderness, poetics, and spirituality, appears in *Shambhala Sun*, *The Wasatch Journal*, and several essay collections.

Raised in an Irish Catholic family, Michael Sowder was trained as a meditation teacher in a tantric yoga tradition in the 1970s and subsequently practiced meditation in Buddhist and Christian mystical traditions. He is the founder of the Amrita Sangha for Integral Spirituality, an organization that explores and teaches the practices of the world's contemplative traditions.